# Drawn
# Parallels

*... then Poetry comes and lays bare the whole landscape with a single splendid flash.*

– Mark Twain

# Drawn Parallels

A Woman's Life in Poetry and Art

JoAnne Bauer

Order this book online at www.trafford.com
or email orders@trafford.com

Most Trafford titles are also available at major online book retailers.

Cover Photograph: JoAnne Bauer, *Back-up Ladies*, 2006.
Interior Images: JoAnne Bauer
Photograph of Author: Robert Fisher

Printed in the United States of America.

Library of Congress Cataloging-in-Publication Data applied for.

ISBN: 978-1-4907-1125-6 (sc)
ISBN: 978-1-4907-1126-3 (e)

*Trafford rev. 05/08/2014*

 www.trafford.com

North America & international
toll-free: 1 888 232 4444 (USA & Canada)
fax: 812 355 4082

# Contents

# I: Double Exposure

## SEEN, BUT NOT HEARD

## Lived Out Loud

# II: Triple Play

## Worth the Price of Admission

# Acknowledgments

I am grateful to the editors of the following publications in which versions of these poems first appeared:

*Avalon Literary Review* (2013): *Ab/solution*

*Bohemia Art and Literary Magazine* (2013): *Ethereal*

*Caduceus* (2013): *Fantastic (Tanfastic)*

*Connecticut River Review* (2013): *Portending Portals*

*Encore* (2012; 2013): *Before the Lesson* and *Wild, in Place*

*Granny Smith Magazine* (2012): *Mother Mine* and *Secret Space, Still*

*Journey to Crone* (Chuffed Buff Books, 2013): *Revived*

*Long River Run* (2011; 2012): *His Service* and *Mapping the Family Farm: 16 Steps*

*Message in a Bottle Poetry Magazine* (2013): *Altering Autumn* and *I Can See Peace*

*Perspectives* (Faxon anthologies 2010; 2011; 2012):
    *Flights of Fancy; haiku; So Close;* and
    *Winter's Morn*

*Poet Tree* (Exiles Press, 2014): *What I Ask*
    and *One July, Contented*

*Poets Against War* (2010): *Redeeming Roses* and
    *Vigilance*

*Rhubarb Magazine* (2012): *... That She Should Be
    Delivered*

*seed packets* (bottle rockets press, 2010): *haiku*

*Theodate* (2012; 2013): *If You Happen Upon ...; Please
    Degas; Sea's Change;* and *Talking Memories*

*30 Day Poetry Challenge Anthology* (2012): *Auto
    Care; blue moon;* and *Forsythia, for You*

*Verse Land* (2013): *Country Remembrance;
    Obit (O Boy); Patterns; Treatment;*
    and *Wedding Day, Mom*

*Where Flowers Bloom* (Grayson Books, 2011):
    *Absorption*

Also by JoAnne Bauer:

Giacquinta, Joseph B., Jo Anne Bauer, and
Jane E. Levin. *Beyond Technology's Promise.*
Cambridge, U.K.: Cambridge University Press, 1993.

*For my Family*
*and Friends*

*Who can tell the dancer from the dance?*

– William Butler Yeats

# I

# Double Exposure

*Caught in Cambridge,* manipulated photograph

*A work of art that did not begin
in emotion is not art.*

– Paul Cézanne

# SEEN, BUT NOT HEARD

*Swept Up in It* (detail), photo transfer with handmade paper

# WEDDING DAY, MOM

Not so very young
yet your face round,
expectant, as you are.

You sit on cement steps
behind Gram's farmhouse;
a frayed braided rug hangs
next to you, awkwardly
from the pipe-railing.

With a splash of color to
the lapel of your navy suit,
poised, formal, you are
posing for this lone photo
before the ceremony.

In your eyes, a trembling –
premonition of what is to come.

## MOTHER MINE

In the hospital, they wrote *'Baby Girl' Bauer;*
the doctor, you said, couldn't hear a heartbeat.

For three pounds-six ounces, no need
to expend a first name, a first love, on one
whose only home might be that incubator.

After two weeks, the birth certificate read *Jo,*
you said, because someone in the bar proposed it.
Male-derived yet, like the heroine of *Little Women,*
imparting female singularity.

Both suspended there and swinging wildly
between a fierce will and choking fear
for life – wanting and not wanting –

headstrong, brooding and immature,
I was and still am your daughter.

# Secret Space, Still

During one of many indoor hours
the young girl discovers
an unfettered, pristine place
to walk, to dream.

Pure white, regal, elegant;
all paths possible.
Her space alone, not touched
or transgressed by anyone.

Holding mom's mirror
under her nose, she steps gingerly
away from the dressing table.

Majestically imagined, she
walks down moulded aisles.
Being alone becomes cherished.
She is princess. No eyes on her.

Transfixed by leaded transoms,
she traverses arched thresholds,
transcends brass light-fixtures,
glides, ever gracefully,
on ceilings.

## WINTER'S MORN

Four of us hand-in-hand
to the bottom of the white hill.
Mom smiles, leading bundles
in snow pants, mittens and caps.

To the bottom of the white hill
a creek runs through Gram's fields.
In snow pants, mittens and caps,
we barely keep from tumbling.

A creek runs through Gram's fields –
narrow, long and frozen.
We barely keep from tumbling
as we skate on double-runners.

Narrow, long and frozen,
our red straps buckled.
As we skate on double runners,
we're pink-cheeked with tingling noses.

Our red straps buckled,
we move in wavy lines.
We're pink-cheeked with tingling noses,
now trudging up the hill.

We move in wavy lines;
Mom smiles, leading bundles
now trudging up the hill,
four of us hand-in-hand.

\*   \*   \*

haiku

home from the hospital –
the memory of gram's morning
glory greets me

## Revived

You withdraw, ignoring me;
I sob and stop breathing.

Flash to that cloistered morning
when the child craved to be heard
by the mother-grandmother matriarchy
that ignored her instinctively, inclined
only toward one another for interchange.

When she slipped unnoticed from their table
and up the stairs to her parents' bedroom,
all that kitchen chatter was mercifully muffled
by the blanket she drew over her head.

With a five-year-old's determination,
pillow to her mouth, she held her breath.
In that moment – for the first time –
she decided to die.

# Mapping the Family Farm: 16 Steps

1
Chase the chickens around the barnyard until
the nasty goose nips your pointer finger.

2
Invite all stuffed animals to a tea party;
borrow Gram's *fancy cups* but don't tell her;
serve flat ginger ale.

3
Bring your Ginny doll, in her homespun
wedding gown, down the meadow when Dad's
two beagles rout out pheasants for shooting.

4
Run like the wind on bowlegs to where
the trapped red fox raided the hen house.

5
Comb dollies' hair with Mommy in her
sewing room; pretend a pregnant reflection
in the stainless handle of the large industrial
flatiron Dad bought for their first anniversary,
which she refuses to use.

6
Skip past Gram's hollyhocks to the draping
mulberry tree, home of your imagined
boyfriend (and his wife and kids).

7
Hide out in the crotch of the sugar maple
as the kitchen oven smolders Wheaties boxes;
build a teepee of old quilts, never to enter
that smoke-stenched house, ever again.
8
Catch butterflies with your cousin;
perfume their wings then watch them
slam into tall six-over-six windows
in the farmhouse bedrooms.
9
Scurry past skunk odor trapped under
the front porch of the farmer's wife who permits
soap-opera viewing every afternoon, 2 pm.
10
Pretend you weren't peering into the
occupied outhouse.
11
Scamper down the sunflower path with Bert;
let him kiss you; don't tell Mommy.
12
Sit five steps up on the walnut staircase
as if you're at the theater and know nothing
about that caterpillar.

13

Crank the *pencil-sharpener-pretend-phone* behind
the kitchen door; place a call to your younger
*brother-husband* chastising him for forgetting
the lima beans on his way from work.

14

Fill the basement with chalk dust trying to
teach the visiting cousin to print a swear word
on the new Christmas-gift blackboard.

15

Push that snow-suited tiny brother as he rolls
a snowball, smiling 'til he tumbles – a snowy
ball himself – into a white drift.

16

Sit very very still, feet dangling off the plush
burgundy couch when Daddy, kissing Mom on the
neck, returns to the family one Sunday afternoon.

## ONE JULY, CONTENTED

I was seven that summer
the tent we played in
was a swamp-green fixture
of the farm's backyard

(a summer before swim lessons,
when the *splashy pool* was grand
and Gram's green beans frolicked
in my mouth at the supper table);

when I almost balanced the two-wheeler
down the path by the fence and did manage
to pump my calves *back and forth,*
*back and forth*, like Daddy shouted
as the swing seat flew skyward,

and when that pungent breath-sucking
smell of army canvas teemed
with my contentment
that two younger brothers
for one brief season

had to make room for me
in their evening revelry,
alongside the Mason Jar lantern
of captive fireflies.

PATTERNS

I drew a white dress with short white gloves,
pillbox hat over bouffant hair.
Jackie Bouvier had A-line flair
and I the urge to copy it.

Pillbox hat over bouffant hair,
setting a tone, upswept a nation;
and I the urge to copy it
with *No. 2* pencil onto lined paper.

Setting a tone, upswept a nation –
youngest president, wife and children.
With *No. 2* pencil onto lined paper,
I wrote my dreams in nascent poems ...

Youngest president, wife and children
daring our hope for Camelot and justice;
I wrote my dreams in nascent poems ...
cut short in Dallas on blood-soaked fabric.

Daring our hope for Camelot and justice,
cut short in Dallas on blood-soaked fabric,
Jackie's veil of darkness flaring;
I drew a black dress with short black gloves.

# BEFORE THE LESSON

*The Dance Class*, 1874
Edgar Degas, oil

A bevy of pubescent girls
gaggling in white tutus;
some swans, others geese.

To the front, neighbor Peg,
pudgy and flatfooted; in dance class
only because her mom said so.

*En pointe*, my best friend Sandy,
center-stage by nature, leans toward
the old master who rests one hand
on his cane, both eyes on her.

Me against the far wall,
withdrawn and sullen – two poses
I already know by heart.

Preening, cackling, fawning, adjusting,
oblivious to joy in movement and naive
about a heritage of wild women dancing,

my mirrored tulle-sisters and I
await promised limelight
and long-stemmed bouquets,
flower petals fluttering ...

## ALTERING AUTUMN

I hadn't gone to the club for weeks;
another swim season winding down
as teens tired of peeling noses
and unlikely romance.

When the Spiegel catalog appeared –
all sage green, mustard seed, burnt orange –
it gave a plaid-and-pleated purpose
to a long Sunday afternoon.

How coordinated I could look
in those mail-order outfits,
starting a new September
the *perfect picture of popular*
to a seventh grade schoolgirl!

Tearing out glossy images,
tape-measuring my waist,
then totaling costs,
I grew gradually deflated:

How could the pitiful thrust
of a new chestnut-colored sweater
remedy what my royal blue, racerback
*Sunday-Style-Section* swimsuit
had failed all the summer long
to redress?

## Fearing Female

Biking Cape Cod trails,
I recall a long-distance trek
one Saturday afternoon
with twelve-year-old friends:

Kathy and Dawn – one's endured
years of breast cancer; the other
succumbed early to the disease.

That day when they invited me
to ride bikes, I was anxious,
but I didn't tell them. I was fearful,
but I didn't let them know.

I didn't tell them I had never ridden
outside our neighborhood;
in fact had never before ridden
my bike off our family lot.

Summers, I'd watch two brothers
pedal away toward friendships,
while I, shy, rode my bike round
and round and round a driveway.

On a mere 50 feet of asphalt,
in sharp turns, I'd imagine I was
the tour winner or a riding instructor,
while parents drank Buds on the back porch.

Outside my comfort zone, straining
to keep pace, I didn't tell my friends;
when I fell and was bleeding,
I didn't let them know.

Later Mom took me to the ER,
a male doc checking my female parts;
I was nervous, but I didn't say so,
frightened, but I didn't let on.

Round and round and round a driveway
in fantasies of preteen prowess;
the legacy of those anxious longings?
Tighter and tighter circles of pretense.

## MEASURED PARENTING

My mom, when I was five,
enjoyed *playing dolls*,
helping me change their diapers
and comb their hair.

Every doll she bought was –
like me – a strawberry blonde.

When I was seven, Mom sewed
tiny outfits for my Ginny –
corduroy pants, a turquoise lounge suit,
the toile-layered wedding gown.

Then at twelve, I began to wonder
*Is she competing with me?*
Her report cards – long archived
in Grandpa's oak desk –
being compared to mine.

By the time I was fifteen,
her Mother's Day corsage
saved in our fridge nosing out
my nosegays …

# DAD

Mom in the kitchen, simmering;
you sit rigid, heavy bear,
as two teen sons
and their older sister
slink around you
in the living room.

The only thread of connection
the shared direction
of our silent stares toward
that evening's line-up
of '60's sitcoms.

*Poetry is a mirror which makes
beautiful that which is distorted.*

– Percy Bysshe Shelley

# LIVED OUT LOUD

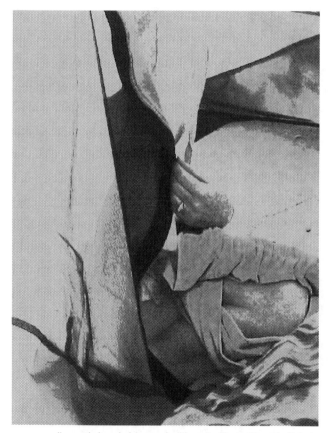

*Recovered*, altered photograph; *Women for Change Alternative Calendar*

## PLEASE DEGAS

*The Tub*, 1884
Edgar Degas, pastel

He cropped it tight, the Artist —
diagonal line from sponge to rear
drawing the viewer's eye across
the paper, over the bather.

A tilted head, unnatural touch
of heels below painfully bent knees;
what we do for art, we models —

Color our hair; scrub a tub;
crouch into an impossible pose
so that the ripple of spine,
the expanse of shoulder muscles,
the flattened hips all catch
early morning sunlight.

I hear you, artist-model.
I hear you question if your
left elbow juts just enough
to counter-balance the reach
of the right; asking for
the next break when you'll sit
ignored on the crimson chair

draped in too thin a shawl,
beseeching: *Maybe, could we*
*adjust those blue curtains so that*
*all of Paris doesn't see me naked,*
*doesn't know how far I'll stoop?*

ONLY I DECIDED
it was rejection …
No one did it, really.

I alone needed that risk
to force me uphill, pushing,
always against gravity toward
the specter of a formidable man –

Clark Kent/the Lone Ranger/ Dr. Bob –
who awes enough to make me
believe in Tinkerbell and ever, ever land
that never, never sustains

yet compels me to surge
straight into his radiance,
blinding both of us
at the moment of impact.

## COUNTRY REMEMBRANCE

Along the route of a foot race
today in Chester CT, floral
fireworks of passion orange
jog her memory ...

On the back of a motorcycle
through PA country roads
that July 4th, she learned
to name them – *Tiger Lilies.*

She never did, though,
speak your name that
same summer, decades ago,

conceiving you mostly
as her one month
of morning sickness.

## Search / Sacrosanct

Group assignment: from a
brainstormed list of words
as to a church, temple, mosque
or cathedral, write about *hunting*

Frantic to find this week's poetry assignment,
I go looking in my *sacristy* of binders –
of poems completed, of notes inchoate.

Hunting furiously at midnight's bells
through pieces of paper, then spires of paper
– cherished papers, blessed papers;

my praise of paper at this hour
turning somber, to disdain of paper.
Then incensed: cursed hypocrisy
of academics! Grab a candle; burn all papers!

Like shouts towards a cathedral vault,
my impatience echoes back to me.
What compels this restlessness –
what stirs from the crypt beneath?

Is it Fear – this heavy organ-drone
on my spirit? Again the child caught
in a dread *confessional* for lost homework?

With time, I find what was missing; then
realize the *true hunt* this task brought me:

To that looking glass – no matter how stained – the sanctuary of reflection through which I eventually discover every emotion I have hidden from myself.

*   *   *

haiku

I tug the myrtle's running roots
to move them –
plans perennially change

# DRAWN IN

*Three Standing Figures*, 1438
Stefano da Verona, pen and ink

Da Verona drew you:
*Standing Figures* in three views.

An ancient art form –
from Paleolithic caves
through Egyptian, Greek,
and Renaissance masters.

I tried my hand at it, with models
of voluptuous curves, muscular angles
or sometimes only rolling flesh.

In cinderblock studios devoid
of color or complexity,
college instructors unwilling
to instruct, instead breezed by, merely
pointing to distorted *negative space* …

Whether gestural or stately,
torsos only; no time
to complete a head or feet.

So I tried my young hand
at figure drawing – an art I loved –
but without encouragement.

*Three Fates,* I see your omen –
cramped forms in static folds,
myopic, decontextualized …

HOW GRATUITOUS saying to me:
*My wife doesn't like you.*

It wasn't I who took your hand
that sultry evening in early May
on the couch of your third floor walk-up,

not noticing darkness descend
before bustling to find, or not,
a light-switch when we heard
furtive footsteps on the stairs.

# If You Happen Upon an Application for a Beauty Pageant: 7 Options

### 1

Fill it out with careful calligraphic script;
reconsider, crumple and swallow whole
with your digestive biscuits

### 2

Soak under water, then shred into
long pieces that you can collage over
your yellowing bedroom walls

### 3

Throw the application into the fire pit
and ceremoniously turn your back
on it at your next shamanic ritual

### 4

Cut out each letter individually;
toss into Campbell's chicken broth
and serve for Sunday supper

### 5

Jog down a race path to the
nearest Port-o-potty; enter and
wrap your application around
the empty toilet paper dispenser

6

Fold several times to fit it in your wallet;
then pray that your handbag gets snapped off
your shoulder and snatched away by a mugger


7

Diligently white-out the typed words
*Beauty* and *Pageant*; hastily replace
with penned words: *Psych* and *Unit*

# To City Evenings

On Market Street
this temperate Thanksgiving eve,
the air thick with melancholy.

*Strawbridge's?* I ask. The fellow
on the corner shakes his head:
*Shut down years back.*

A stopover haven near the subway station,
that department store had been my source
for many last-minute holiday gifts
– oh, and colorful bowls for my NYC co-op.

Gimbels, Lit Brothers, Wanamakers,
all festive emporiums in the Christmas season,
had been all I knew of Philadelphia
– oh, and an automat for dinner once,
in late autumn.

Shopping then, my mom chose for me
a forest-green, wool winter coat;
a bit too dark, too large, too long
for my small frame and fair skin.

Back then, all I knew of Philadelphia
was that one shopping trip
– oh, and the oft-repeated story about
her late teen years when, my mother claimed,

she routinely drove her girlfriends
from PA farm life to *the big city*
in her bright yellow convertible.

Now I, too, choose bright colors
and big cities; but not girlfriends.
No, not girlfriends.

I do not trust them, as
I could not trust my mother.

$$*\quad*\quad*$$

## It's Christmas

Time for the age-old lesson:
not to measure our worth
by other people's limitations.

# Drawing Scorn

*Lucretia*, 1512
Raphael, pen and ink

Unfamiliar with your legend
Lucretia, I view you in folds
of fabric, elegantly posed as if
your only purpose was pure portrayal

by Raphael and fellow figure-artists
who drew you with wistful gaze
falling toward your future …
But with one breast exposed,
as if you beckoned the boy …

I read that your story swirled
such unspeakable scandal as to fell
the monarchy of mighty Rome;

that on a night of your husband's absence
in brute battle for his king would come the son
to your bedroom, despoiling all Honor …

You with broad hips Lucretia, and
voluptuous beauty so belying defilement …
Woman! Were you raped a second time
by History, and a third by Art …?

Your dagger, disguised in a glint of chalk,
drawn as if protection; not rendered true
to the bloody blade you would thrust –
out of unfathomable shame –
into your own heart.

# Not Ready

Tears well up;
eyes swell.
Tugs to the heart
start the morning.

Eyes swell;
lids close.
Start the morning
without compassion.

Lids close;
breath heaves.
Without compassion
I meditate.

Breath heaves
in and out.
I meditate
into silence.

In and out,
tugs to the heart.
Into silence,
tears well up.

## … THAT SHE SHOULD BE DELIVERED

A holiday for her release
but what price to be exacted on return?

She carries a 17-year-old Walkman,
a 20-year-old nylon bag,
a $7.99 drugstore camera
that won't focus in overcast light,
and plastic wraparound sunglasses
free from the optician.

She takes the bus to Providence
with bustling masses …

On this, the day after Christmas
she feels ready to claim deliverance,
take to the road, get out of town
to escape from you
and the currency of
the presentless present.

## Major Stressors, Compressing

How do you write about
chronic pain that twisted
your every day for more
than a decade?

Head pain that sought out
every treatment imaginable?

Do you say you forgave
the mugger his bleak, drug-induced
need to snatch your handbag

but not your *significant other*
his foibles, screeched about daily
in the streets, pubs, parks of NYC?

Do you mention that three professors,
who should have known better,
fought another turf-war at your
doctoral orals the prior afternoon?

And that your dad died six weeks
before that, your mom a year earlier?

Or that a brother's comment
at the family estate-sale
the previous weekend displaced
all sense of belonging, all grounding ...

# TREATMENT

You forced me – or
did I force you to drag me –
to the hospital that desolate night,
somewhere before Easter
somewhere before *I think*
*I smothered my baby brother* ...

And before the shackles in
that dark room where disembodied
faces (straining to restrain me)
each emerged as characters in
a screenplay my mind went scribbling.

Where are those notes ...
my master *oeuvre*
stuffed in metal drawers?
Why do we never talk about my trek,

that fathomless, arduous journey
to a high-ground retreat, beyond
white-coated doctors forcing meds,
an OT room with orange birdhouses,

and through dark choral clouds
of psych nurses endlessly entreating:
*Why are you so paranoid?*
*What is wrong with you?*

## Full Plate/Served

Stretched beyond rational limits,
I'm asked again to look
the other way, second-guess myself,
let it slide *just this once.*

*No*, I say. *Not this time!*

I will no longer tolerate:
lawyers who lie,
insurance reps who don't pay
or fine print that misleads.

It. is. a. new. day.

Make note: I will take no prisoners,
agree to no concessions;
will refuse to negotiate,
and when necessary, bring charges.

But different from what I get from you,
you will receive notice from me –
upfront, in plain English, and with font size
big enough for any jaundiced eye to read!

*Study the past if you would define the future.*

– Confucius

# II

# Triple Play

*Unmasking Her Ways* ...., emulsion photographic transfer

*... we are every one of us a poet
when we are in love.*

– Plato

# WORTH THE PRICE OF ADMISSION

*Beginnings*, paper collage

# TALKING MEMORIES

*Grainstacks in Bright Sunlight*, 1890;
Claude Monet, oil

It was excessive expense for us, I recall,
that summer of our European *vacances*
a month before I moved to Manhattan;
how I planned to speak French to locals
in advance of grad school's language exam.

Amidst the Eiffel Tower, Heidelberg's castle
or snow-covered peaks in August's Alps,
what I remember most are the lazy fields
in sunlit southern France,

with ubiquitous rolls of hay,
stacks of gold grains, and olive trees
against an azure haze of hills –

long, long, long expanses
in our rental car heading toward Paris,

you and I barely speaking ...

## TIGER-EYED

### 1
Midnight jacket, smoky tie,
black shirt; deft fingers
button his collar.

### 2
Each performance practiced,
repeated, perfected; yet
one thread unraveling –

### 3
From a backstage door, fleeing
down the dark alleyway; finally
unbuttoned from the Master.

## PORTENDING PORTALS

If, on the wall of your heart
I had sketched a ladder,
climbed up and peered over,

I'd have noticed in the galley kitchen
your daughter's apron strings,
your ex-wife's meatloaf recipe,
your son's empty Coors cans.

If I'd pulled myself passed the sill
of your heart's window, I'd have seen
Disney World photos, heard Buffet tunes,
or read cousin Jeanette's letter
pleading that you move south.

Instead I invited you across
the threshold of my urban Victorian,
played Telemann flute sonatas,
introduced you to male poet friends.

At my carriage house hearth,
I served sweet crepes and shared
with you my sexual appetite.

From a curious balcony, your
close-up and wide-angle aperture
disrobed the sunlit differences
that, in the end, made all the difference.

## LEAVES

Each time I go out of town alone,
I wonder how you'll greet me on return.

Last July to Boston, wide-eyed
for *Whitman and Arts Literacy*
at a brick-and-ivy college;

you, on the morning I left,
misinterpreting my words,
heard their exact opposite.

During my entire absence,
in jealousy-knotted ire
you refused all phone calls,

instead sending anguished e-mails
that I jogged across campus
during lunch breaks to decipher.

This August in Northampton
I visit friends, again study art.

In the bookbinding studio
at a table far from classmates, I
ponder the bond between you and me:
Is it mystery that conjoins us?

Or are we bound by fantasies
that you craft, confused in fictions
that abridge my distinct voice

yet bind me to you as surely as
the clamp holding these book covers
now in rigid tightness,

while I watch glue harden
around delicate silken strands.

## AB/SOLUTION

On your laptop amidst folders,
inside one labeled *Reference*,
six snapshots of a blonde.

From each middle-aged jpeg
smiling, she could be my sister.
She's not, though; nor yours.

Recall that summer afternoon
Mom snatched me from the backyard
to reveal a photo of a woman in
fur-collared dress and open-toed shoes,
saying *I found this in your dad's suit pocket.*

Back then a confidante of suspicions,
my nine-year-old mind now clicks
on your keyboard a new option,
the necessary choice:
*Clear History.*

## WHAT I ASK

Against the hedges farthest
from the farmhouse eyes
stood the mulberry bush;
so tall I called it a tree and
huddled under its draping bosom.

My buddies lived there,
always home, always
feasting on the mulberries.

Eager playmates they, ready to
climb with me when I said to climb,
and jump with me if I needed to jump,
or cry with me when I pleaded to cry.

Now, in sunset questions
of our grownup summer:
did I require such blind devotion
from you also, my lover
(and imagined friend)?

## AUTO CARE

My Dodge, stolen one night
right under my nose.
Lucky thief in the distance
claimed what was mine.

Right under my nose
a lock broke months back –
claimed what was mine –
I'm forced to admit.

A lock broke months back;
I paid little heed
I'm forced to admit,
from a rearview mirror.

I paid little heed
to my care of my car.
From a rearview mirror
I see now how the trespass

to my care, of my car
started with me, cavalier …
I see now how the trespass
– as with my lover –

started with me, cavalier.
Lucky thief in the distance
– as with my lover …
my Dodge, stolen one night.

# Ex/hibition

On two walls hang my poetry and art;
yours grace opposite sides of Salt Gallery.

Months ago we planned and scheduled
this, our summer showcase. When we
altered publicity to read: *2 One-person Shows,*
it seemed a tidy fix.

You near your art; I next to mine,
no longer the *person,* the me, who
built assemblages, crafted poetic phrases.

Yet friends congregate and linger,
offer compliments appreciative, giddy.

In this artistic aftermath of our
relationship's dissolve, would I feel less
dissociated, depressed, disowned
if fewer had come to witness our exhibit
of vulnerability?

## To Matter

I bought the dollhouse one December
a few weeks before Christmas.
You and I were living together,
or so I thought, as I used
the familiarity and order
of your one-floor apartment
to rationalize my life.

That was the end of a year
when we pondered whether you
would move into my big house,
or buy us a home in the suburbs,
or you a place deep in the woods
and me a townhouse in another city.

With colored lights on its rooftop
and next to Raggedy Ann and Marvin,
it anchored the *toy room* of our festivities
and fourth shared Christmas.

My dollhouse remained at your home
for the next year and a half, through
a new round of holiday parties
and apparent domesticity.

Today, after another year has passed
and you are moving away,
you found and delivered to me
one more of the tiny tumblers
from the brass tray on the sideboard
in the dollhouse dining room.

So diminutive those tumblers,
so easily overlooked;
yet all six recovered.

*Matter is never lost*, they say. *Never.*
*Neither destroyed nor created.*

I wonder now:
Is that also true of love?

# haiku

a young girl
ties queen anne's lace
round the barn cat's neck


clip a wild rose branch
to carry indoors –
petals cascade


two gardenias grace
the plant you gave me –
you are getting married

# In October

Oh sure, I usually prefer
brilliant sunlight
through mirror-blue skies.

But let's not underestimate
the romance of a rainy
Vermont afternoon.

Against pitch-dark tree trunks,
striated rock outcrops,
the occasional stately birch

in extended twilight mist,
orgasmic foliage colors –
apricot, persimmon, caramel ...

Autumn my lover now.

Alas, Siddhartha, I see you suffering, but you're suffering a pain at which one would like to laugh, at which you'll soon laugh for yourself.

– *Hermann Hesse*

# MAKING FUN, NATURALLY

*Return Trip*, collage postcard

# Early June

In full moonlight,
honeysuckle scent
into my bedroom
dreams of adolescence.

Honeysuckle scent
climbing the porch trellis.
Dreams of adolescence –
you kiss me.

Climbing the porch trellis
livid clematis flowers;
you kiss me,
tendrils entwining.

Livid clematis flowers
into my bedroom;
tendrils entwining
in full moonlight.

## Goodwill Hunting

Ignorant of orthodox ways
when the Jewish academy
hired me to direct pupil services,
I startled at their dress code:
knee length or longer – I owned none!

End of summer sales pulled me
toward consignment shops where
volunteer ladies of *elegant* age commanded:
*Take that doggone designer dress;*
*we can't get rid of stuff your size!*

At home, bliss spread across my sofa;
jackets paired with shirts, sweaters
to scarves, I was a *girl* again,
playing with clothes.

A decade marked by second-hand treasures
keeping me from maws of malls
yielded six closets of unique creations
with outlandish flair.

At ten bucks per forty-gallon trash bag,
I stuffed in fifty items and then some.
To routine compliments, I'd quip:
*These skirts cost less than the hangers that hold them!*

# FORSYTHIA, FOR YOU

Forsythia each spring reminds me
April fools we were
on your birthday, dressed as jesters
to a sunrise vigil.

April fools we were,
*Raggedy Ann and Andy* redheads
to a sunrise vigil;
*bookends* they called us.

*Raggedy Ann and Andy* redheads
matching Earth Shoes and purple shirts
– *bookends* they called us –
strolling to the tennis courts.

Matching Earth Shoes and purple shirts
in first live-together love,
strolling to the tennis courts
holding each other's hearts.

In first live-together love
on your birthday, dressed as jesters
holding each other's hearts –
Forsythia each spring reminds me.

## Fantastic (Tanfastic)

At lunch she beams her summer color.
*It's fake; a 'Hollywood Tan,'* my friend
confides, *and it covers my whole body!*
Lifting elbows, Sarah shows off
underarms as bronze as her face.

*What about risks?* I query;
fair-skinned with freckles
and childhood sunburns, I've
been indoctrinated to fret over
sunspots, lesions, dread cancer.

A blank stare is her reply
and all I need to know.
In that instant, I see Sarah
suspended in a mythic state of grace –

driving a sky-blue convertible,
popping in for pedicures
and frequenting the salon –
a day-to-day as fanciful for me
as that perfect summer tan.

# Recounting

Planning for a collage course
out of town in August,
I searched the Chamber directory
for accommodations.

Without warning, your name
and address appeared,
my wild lover of 36 years ago;
I haven't seen you for 35.

A therapist now, back then you
were a student of metaphysics
and a reciter of poems.
(Weren't we all scholars of life and love,
on that cloistered seminary campus?)

Now in the hotel pool, I anticipate
a lunch-meeting with you,
memories swimming through my mind.

Memories – daunting,
like pool laps, intentions in motion;

Memories – breathtaking,
like laps, arousing ripples;

Memories – like these laps I count,
counting on them, surely, to end.

# Seasons of Tea

*Tea Stories – Other Worlds*, 2012
Carolyn Q. Tertes, mixed media

*Noon* (Summer)

tufts of amber hay mounding;
robust sunflowers, tall as a ladder,
crown his straw hat

*Evening* (Autumn)

ochre fans twirl on twigs – fall;
a butternut moon full
glistens her empty cup

*Night* (Winter)

vanilla wisps above
pewter storm clouds;
lamppost snow froths my mug

*Dawn* (Spring)

sunrise flings a peach signature
on budding hills; fiery
filaments fly from maples

## New Ground

I say yes to your invitation to dance.
Foxtrots on hardwood; your cocky smile
still familiar after four years of no contact.

A week later, you phone again:
*Could we meet on Memorial Day?*
You offer a picnic; I'll bring poetry.

Though you don't mention it,
I know this to be an anniversary.

Our first picnic with poetry
was Memorial Day nine years ago,
shortly after our first smiling; but
I was troubled, and you were scared.

Five years later, again for private poetry;
you in silent pain and I asking myself
why I bothered to still know you.

Today is different:
no wants; known limits.

Making peace with a friendship,
you and I in unison stand
to pull the patchwork quilt
ahead of ourselves,
again into mottled sunlight.

# FLIGHTS OF FANCY

Some poems –
winged words – land easy;
like a recent flight,
blue skies and friendly crew.

Winged words – land easy
as arrival in Ireland;
blue skies and friendly crew,
baggage already circling.

As arrival from Ireland,
others in turbulence;
baggage already circling,
jolted, and purged.

Others in turbulence
sputtering unease;
jolted and purged
toward a choppy landing.

Sputtering unease,
like a recent flight
toward a choppy landing
– some poems.

# True Feat

Thank you, Coach Brent,
for your simple act of stringing
that make-shift finish line Sunday
across the road, marking our end
of three months' summer training.

With the half-marathon group,
trudging toward orange crepe paper,
I instinctively raised my arms.
Legs tired since mile 9 burst
forward in fresh determination.

Because of your gesture
I grabbed a *second wind*, running
on and on, Forest Gump-like
up the steep hill, past

trees and streams, 'round
and 'round and 'round the reservoir,
sweating, aching, pushing
to a new *personal best* – 26.2 –

my first marathon triumph!

# First Light

*Bridge over a Pond of Water Lilies*, 1899
Claude Monet, oil

My timid foray into online dating:
It's a good sign, I think, when you suggest
our afternoon at the city's athenaeum.

Monet in special exhibition, and
we're transported to blue-green
pleasantries of Giverny gardens.

You comment about paint hues,
leave impressions gossamer
as willows in dappled sunlight.

Catching my eye, a bridge
of unknown substance spans
a uncertain distance over lily pads —

without apparent beginning
or endpoint in sight,
perhaps leading nowhere,

winsome in its presence …

## So Close

How different this early jaunt
from yesterday's when the sky
was a cerulean field of possibility.
A humid-gray pall dampens our routine.

Reservoir workmen displace serenity,
with weed whackers, trees axes,
riding mowers that buzz, echo and snort.

Diesel-fuel stench invades nostrils
as our legs drone heavy on
through air already thick and slow.

Unexpected, at the edge of the woods
near the pond wafts honeysuckle fragrance.
Intoxicating; morning molasses meets us,
and we are welcomed alive again.

## SEA'S CHANGE

*The Great Wave at Kanagawa*, 1831
Katsushika Hokusai, wood block print

Three brothers in the stateroom next to ours
yelp, as if flying round the first curve
of the wooden roller coaster at Sylvan Beach.

You and I on our side of the wall lie still
in bed, groaning middle-aged midnight moans
as the ship bounds forward over turbulence,

wondering in the dark how
a mirror-smooth sea turned fiendish,
betraying a naiveté about cruises
and our sense of measured safety.

The silver-plated trash receptacles that
at first glance were mocked as middlebrow,
we now pull – one to your side of the bed,
the other to mine – closer to our chins.

## WILD, IN PLACE

I like to jog past our neighbor's house
on the corner of our street.
We watched him, remember,
when he was sowing the seeds.

A *meadow* of wildflowers
now bursts from the middle
of his rectangled lawn:

*Cosmos, pink; cornflowers, blue;*
*poppies, orange; daisies, too.*
*Queen Anne's Lace or sunflowers, tall;*
*I wish I could name them all!*

The irony of those wildflowers
is not lost on me, contained
within a suburban fence
of pickets and barbed wire.

Yet look there, at the curb in
the vertex of asphalt and concrete.

On both sides of the street
two innocent sprouts
in rebellious freedom;
mirrors of tenacity and survival.

# It was Snowing; I was Mowing

Predictions popped to my awareness
at the last minute –
early October blizzard, with
russet leaves still on branches …

*Perfect storm* of disaster:
Nor'easter that felled
aged trees and power lines,
left me with no heat
for a week, no phones for two.

I marvel now how heedlessly
I sat reading polemics
glazed-eyed at my monitor
while around me sloppy snow
cracked limbs, peppered the night.

Did I store in food?
Water? A generator?
Batteries, lantern, or ice?

Nary a preparation did I make except
a last seasonal swipe at overgrown grass,
mowing my lawn at noon as first flakes fell.

Next time, I vow I'll be more
prac-ti-cal; next time, ahead of time,
I will wash my hair!

## ABSORPTION

It's begun raining
as I grab your daughter's bike;
five miles my goal today
in triathlon training.

Rain spatters
your goldenrod slicker
that reaches mercifully
past my knees.

Droplets gleam
the handlebars
and pitter-patter
my helmet *harpsichord.*

Tires striking wet asphalt
reverberate the distance.

Beyond my dewy-wet glasses
are fields of watercolor greens
and rosebuds melting into Monet's.

Rain-soaked – my routine
a wash of reverie – I decide
to pedal these park paths again,
one extra/ordinary time.

NOV in NYC,
traditional as turkey;

leaves of red-rust hue
linger through CPW.

A spring in my step reminds:
my love affair remains

\*    \*    \*

BLUE MOON
radiant sphere
searing a purple sky
fully glowing luminous orb
midnight

# NEW MORN

Four a.m. stillness;
a robin chisels sound
through summer's dark.

Ochre-flashing digital time;
too early to be this eager –
still, clarity trumping fear,
I find resolve in first light.

Didn't the Tarot reader tell me:
*You can take the long way 'round;*
*but what if there were an easy path,*
*a shortcut, a new approach?*

Skipping out and back with mirth,
straight to a target. Letting go the angst,
the pondered meandering from far-reaches ...

... who lives so near the stars as I, or who so near the depths of the abyss?

– Friedrich Nietzsche

# ALL FALL DOWN

*Taos – for Hasu*, construction paper collage

# VIGILANCE

This Fourth of July to a peace vigil,
I pedal my usual route through
West Hartford's cemetery.

In the distance over treetops,
a lifeguard's whistle signals
a storm closer than
allowed for swimming.

Thick air – alternating now
between gusts and stillness –
disturbs regimented rows
of miniature grave flags.

Heavy-hearted, the sky
blasts a shattering howl.

Beyond the stone wall
where the road bends, I brake
into tears for innocents lost.

## About Olives, Mr. Hall

on reading Donald Hall's
poem *Olives**

Photos fall from their album sleeves,
pile up at my scanner. Our high school
reunion looms, as I fill the class *Facebook* page
with innocent snapshots:

Editor of yearbook kissing
editor of school newspaper
(one of three girls he is taller than)
at ninth grade graduation party

Head cheerleader (in bright turquoise heels)
laughing on lap of basketball captain
in rec room of her dad, the Assistant Principal

Homecoming queen with blonde bouffant
reaching long white gloves toward
elbow of her date, the football QB

*Class poet* (who arrived in tenth grade
as instant heartthrob for all *academic* girls)
pouring pitcher of Pabst over salutatorian
for declining to marry him

Forty years' toll:

Our head cheerleader, class president,
hockey captain, and class treasurer,
all refusing to be found

A student council senior one year after graduation
shot in his bathtub over a failed drug deal

Our Ph.D. cancer researcher taken
by a tumor soon after publishing his book

The Annette Funicello look-alike since grade two,
so ravaged from donating a kidney to her niece,
refused to leave home for her last five years

These and others from my class –
a suicide, breast cancer statistics,
Vietnam casualties, motorcycle carnage –
know whether *the dead don't like olives*, Mr. Hall;

What they'll never know is *wheezing upstairs – obese
halfbacks beside cheerleaders waiting for hip replacements
– while a doddering poet … cavorts with their daughters\**
in lascivious license, anywhere he can imagine.

## A Woman Has Needs

At a public library workshop
in the week before Christmas,
you approach, interrupting us.

Hanging from your ears,
round silvery bells, gaudy
enough in pairs; yet ten
each larger than the one above
fall onto the hot yellow of your jacket
over the bright pink of your jeans.

When you open your mouth,
your words falter, sputter, stutter,
delay me; disturbing my field of vision,
my conversation, my train of thought.

*Where ... where ...*
*where ...*
*where ...*
*are ... the ... jobs?*

Watching your words hang
helplessly in air, I try
to not appear impatient

like that driver who had to wait
until the young woman she hit
at the corner of Park and Marshall

rolled off her hood and walked
out of the intersection
away from her white Honda,
before proceeding west to her
suburban home for dinner.

At midnight alone in bed,
through the dark I see
those silvery bells,
dangling wet
from my eyes.

# ANALOGY (AFGHANISTAN)

upon viewing the
documentary film, *Restrepo*

Memorial Day race:
start all infants at the base
of Avon Mountain for their
crawl-contest to the summit.

Only one can be victorious,
ascendant prizewinner,
with laurels glorious!

Supply them with visors
and baby food – if you choose –
but know that will slow their mission.

Flags? Of course. Blue, white and
red stakes to claim dominion
and forever mark their trails
of conquest and blood.

Forbid cannibalism?
Hmm, I think not. They will be hungry,
and by the time our babies return,
all party food and spirits

will have been devoured by patrons
and parents who picnicked all day long
in the pavilion, shaded from the blazing sun …

# Obit (O Boy)

*More than enough romance for*
*any woman*, begins her obituary;
she had every man she ever wanted …

Well, maybe one slithered off
sideways, without a whimper.

The others finally fell out the front door
past tears of remorse and pleading.

None took anything as he left –
not an album, anniversary gift,
not even the four-corner poster bed
passed down from his grandparents.

Breathing in as they breathed out
rhythmically – slow inhale, exhale;
pull, push, then hold –
she loved each one, madly.

Fiercely. Desperately;
as if that tantric in-breath
were her only Breath.

## Ragged/Way Home

Jason is dying …
Four cats scurry from
new feet, busy in his kitchen
near their water bowl.

Jason is dying …
At home. *Last stages,*
the hospice nurse declares.

Someone snaps a Russian sage sprig
from his garden, holds it to his nose.
*Too much,* he bristles, senses stripped.

Another assures he's going to heaven.
Jason shakes his head, as atheist friends
scowl in whispered uproar.

A former lover wants Jason's teeth in;
his neighbor sure they're pinching him
while the VA buddy growls, *Leave him alone.*

Jason is dying …
What made sense yesterday
no longer belongs.

Write an obituary or not,
dust his pottery or not,
email an update or not,

Jason is dying ...
shrinking to skeleton.

We keep vigil, watch mortality,
blast out displaced grief;
struggling to know
what we cannot, to fathom
this: dying.

# LOVE LETTING

*Love Letters in the Sand**
Coots and Kenny, 1931

One afternoon near the end
of her six-year cancer,
my mom requested
I wheel her to the piano.

*On a day like today we'd pass the time away ...*

With fingers hitting keys
in no apparent sequence,
still her favorite song
echoed from her heart's-voice.

*You made a vow that you would ever be true*

After she died that April,
there were some surprises –
revelations, really.

In the long bureau drawer
next to her twin bed
that had taunted our dad

*But somehow that vow meant nothing to you*

were nine bathing suits,
deliberately folded and stacked
to hide their fade marks

*Now my broken heart aches with every wave that breaks ...*

and a tiny velvet gift box
holding the younger woman's
double-hearted locket.

---

\*    *Love Letters in the Sand* (music by J. Frederick Coots with lyrics by Nick
and Charles Kenny), first published in 1931 and made popular by
singer-idol Pat Boone, for whom it was a 1957 gold record hit.

ETHEREAL

You arrived as a ball of fluff,
bouncing in all directions.

A kitten, your smile
enigmatic yet unmistakable
whenever you sat puff-chested
in sunlight at my dorm window.

Neither leash nor tall tree thwarted you,
wily free. Camouflaged on a branch,
not easy, not too hard to coax down.

We tossed your bright yarn ball, which
you'd unravel back to solid colors
then look away, wanting to be noticed
again and again, yet again.

On high kitchen shelves you feigned innocence,
then haunched down to attack. We'd chastise
yet snap photos all the same.

In your dotage, holiday scarves round your neck,
you scratched at legs under the dining table
yet always ducked clear of wayward feet.

The world was cuddle-warm, simpler,
yet full lovable, Ti, when you were here.

## CUSTOMER

As bright pink as azaleas
announcing another April
was the lightweight work jacket
my dad bought for himself.

After Mom died, my brothers
and I watched him –
ever the reluctant shopper –
try on solitary decision-making
and a new-found fashion freedom.

On the phone that second spring,
he sought a daughter's opinion:
*If you like that jacket, Dad, why not?*

The following February on
the rainy afternoon of his funeral
– as was custom – we invited
relatives to the family house.

In the coat closet off the entry foyer,
unsettling as bright bouquets
over a casket, hung his pink jacket.

Purchased, but my dad had never used it;
in the end, his well-worn habits
– like its sales tag – remaining intact.

## His Service

On a whim today, I *google* the name
of a former friend who came to mind.
(This an ego-indulgence, wondering
in the inevitable comparisons of
professional lives who will come up short.)

A dedicated high school teacher, twenty years ago
Seth followed me to New York. On his leaving
CT, students showered him with gifts
(and I envied how beloved he was).

He to Columbia, I to NYU, for doctoral degrees
and whatever a big city would offer us.
Markedly successful, Seth on graduation
became an Associate Dean.

In periodic lunches on the Upper West Side,
we traded stories about our fathers who both
died that frigid February, fifteen years ago.

Many holidays after I moved from NY,
Seth and I exchanged letters; then
transitions brought lost contact and
unreliable updates from friends.

Expectant now, I search the Internet
anticipating articles, perhaps photos
of Seth in academia.

Eager at the first reference:

*Seth, Dean, beloved*        (of course!)
*by students and colleagues ...*

                      (envious)

*remembered on campus*
*in a public service ...*

                      (paused)

*He succumbed from injuries ...*

                      (numb)

*suffered in a car accident.*
*Seth was 49.*

                      (crushed)

## Redeeming Roses

Five years after 9/11, in a gathering
of stunned community, we met an artist
who unveiled his canvas of
that devastated mourning.

An anguished innocence
captured the ungraspable.
Onlookers again, we relived
the ravages of that day
rendered in anointed oils …

Ten years later, the horror billows wider;
molten roses defy our watchful eyes.
We cannot outrun the blue sky turned ashen,
nor escape terrored towers in free fall.

Children, caught in blinding-white
lies, we have tripped over bodies
of evidence. At first hidden,
then re-covered, shreds of
crumpled truth rivet our gaze.

And victims' cries grow fiercer,
now worldwide, relentlessly rebuking us:
to rescue our own lives,
our hardened hearts, in denial
of the cold blood
still falling
on our mired hands.

# PYRRHIC

The preacher proclaims
his death a Victory.
For you? Still the mother
of your fifty-year-old son

who shrank to half his size
in less than seven weeks;
no longer robust, his body
clad in cancer and walnut.

From many pews back,
there are moments
I don't see your ebony hat
arrayed, sometimes askew.

*No mother should ever bury
a son*, you told me yesterday.
Emphatically. Yet here we sit.

*Oh, Death, where thy sting?*
the preacher crows;
my eyes whisper: *I know.*

## I Can See Peace

Find our place
of gentle miracles –
I'll meet you there –

where anger crackles
like logs spent to a fire;
where tribes realign,

nature's beauty adds wisdom,
breezes carry compassion,
and vision dims to mere sunlight.

Our task must be to free ourselves
by widening our circle of
compassion to embrace all living
creatures and the whole of
nature and its beauty.

– Albert Einstein

# Afterword

Except for scraps of verse in adolescence, my poetry writing began in earnest when I took a workshop with Sarah Pemberton Strong in 2007. Sarah responded: *I like the way I'm able to fill in more than you give me on the page; that creates overtones extending beyond the poem. A good example of how knowing what to leave out is as important as what to leave in ... wonderful work this week.* Immediately, I scribbled a handful more poems, then a hiatus.

By 2009, I had written enough to sit down one summer morning with my friend Lonnie Black to share our poetry. A significant and formative exchange for me, with Lonnie declaring: *You're a poet. You're there!*

After that, I attended a haiku workshop with Stanford Forrester, sponsored by Marilyn Johnston and Wintonbury Library in Bloomfield and soon thereafter received notice of my first publication – haiku – in *seed packets* by bottle rockets press.

By 2010, I had found a home with the Faxon poetry group of West Hartford and was included in their *Perspectives IV* anthology, annually compiled by Steve Olechna. In 2011, I became publicity coordinator for the statewide Connecticut Poetry Society and a regular member of their Hartford

Chapter meetings. Throughout 2012, I was honored with poetry prizes in state contests and many small press publications.

The project that eventually became this manuscript started two years ago when a companion, knowing I'm a visual artist and an appreciator of all things cultural, gave me a holiday gift of a daily art calendar (workman.com). Each day of the new year, the gift calendar presented me with artwork from the vast collection of the Metropolitan Museum in New York City.

Immediately, I decided ekphrasis was in order, and I set about to write a poem-a-day, in response to the daily image. That endeavor lasted exactly two weeks when I realized that such a schedule was much too ambitious to fit into an already busy lifestyle. However, I continued to find the images inspiring and especially helpful in my quest to finish poems that had, until then, eluded completion.

In the Appendix, the reader will find an alphabetical index of poem titles, alongside the list of identified artwork that motivated, mirrored, and challenged my writing. Most are from the Met; several others are from Hill-Stead Museum in Farmington and the New Britain Museum of American Art, CT; and a few are from other well-known art collections.

The poetry circle of Greater Hartford continues to engage me – with monthly feedback from Faxon and CPS buddies; readings at Word Forge; annual social justice poetry at the Harriet Beecher Stowe House sponsored by Riverwood Poets; Pond House readings from *Friends and Enemies of Wallace Stevens;* and of course, internationally known poets in the Sunken Garden of Hill-Stead each summer.

My heartfelt and abiding gratitude extends to
this enlivening circle and especially to:
Sarah Pemberton Strong, Lonnie Black, the Faxon
Poets and Marcia Lewis, Dale Batchelder, Brad Davis
and Theodate, the Connecticut Poetry Society,
Ginny Connors, Rennie McQuilken, Melody Moore,
Donna Fleischer, Cliff Emery, Marilyn Johnston,
the Free Poets Collective and Colin Haskins,
Tony Fusco, Pat Mottola, Jim Finnegan, Rhett Watts,
Doreen Stern, Christine Beck, Tom Nicotera,
Jerry Howard, and all my poetry-loving friends. – JB

IX
When the blackbird flew out of sight,
It marked the edge
Of one of many circles.

– Wallace Stevens

# *Appendix*

This appendix alphabetically lists all book poems alongside inspiring artwork, unless otherwise specified, from the Metropolitan Museum of Art, New York City.

*I tore myself away from the safe comfort ... through my love for truth — and truth rewarded me.*

– Simone de Beauvoir

# About the Author

JoAnne Bauer, Ph.D., holds a doctorate from New York University in Communication Arts and Technology and advanced degrees in special education leadership, psychology of religion and philosophy.

A self-styled *Renaissance woman*, she has been honored as a special education director and for her nonprofit leadership, environmental activism, scholarship and research, events coordination and promotion, mixed media visual art, photography, video camerawork, grant-making, and poetry.

While living in New York City and leading a successful social justice coalition, JoAnne became dedicated to building community. Since 2006, she has completed marathons, triathlons and half-marathons for charitable causes as well as participated in a fundraising pageant, during which she was tickled to be voted *Ms. Congeniality*.

Co-author of *Beyond Technology's Promise* (Cambridge University Press, 1993), JoAnne presented research articles at national conferences and taught academic writing. She also served as an associate editor and reviewer for professional journals. Her poetry has received state prizes and small press acceptances regionally, nationally and abroad, including a chapbook by *Finishing Line Press*.

JoAnne lived her first nine years on Gram's farm in Pennsylvania, a decade in Manhattan and Brooklyn, has traveled widely, and now is delighted to reside in the historic West End of Hartford CT, where Wallace Stevens also walked and wrote poetry.